How to Prune an Apple Tree

A guide for real people with imperfect trees

Chloe Ward

Why I wrote this booklet

Sometimes it seems I can't walk down the street without someone asking me how to prune their fruit trees. Over the last ten years I've taught many people how to prune fruit, so I know that real, ordinary people can learn to do it. Yet, there seems to be a lack of written information on pruning that is understandable to the non professional. This guide is my attempt to meet that need. I've done my best to demystify pruning, and I very much hope it will empower the real person to prune his/her tree with confidence.

My experience of fruit growing is mostly in Kent (at Yalding Organic Gardens) and in mid Wales (at the Centre for Alternative Technology) and as a freelance gardener and consultant. Although I have written with the UK climate in mind, the principles and techniques should apply to apple (and pear) trees growing anywhere in a temperate climate.

I am indebted to Hugh Ermen (1928 – 2009), fruit expert, apple breeder and 'own-root' fruit tree pioneer, who gave me a real understanding of pruning when I was fortunate enough to receive his wisdom during his last few years in Kent. Also to his wife Laura Ermen. Both Hugh and Laura were always generous with their time and encouragement.

Thank you to all who commented on my drafts – Claire, Julie, Sarah, Candy, Jon, Leigh, Rick, Maggie, Stefan, Gabi, Teg, Catherine, Sally, Fi, James, Ann, Sue, Lynn, Sam, Stella, and especially to Catriona for proof-reading. Any mistakes are my own.

First Published 10th March 2014 by Create Space independent publishing

This edition published October 2016 by Chloe Ward

Printed in Llandysul by Gomer Press Ltd on FSC certified paper

Cover Design by Annika Faircloth

FSC www.fsc.org MIX Paper from responsible sources FSC® C114687

Contents

How to Prune an Apple Tree

Every winter, people look at their fruit trees with a mixture of concern and bafflement. Most of us have an idea that apple trees need pruning. The tree may look out of shape, or perhaps hasn't been fruiting well, but performing surgery on our trees is rightly nerve-racking – how do we know that our pruning will have the desired effect?

The fruit trees we have in our back gardens have their own histories and individual quirks. They are not like those in commercial orchards, or show gardens. They are unique and need treating accordingly. Because all trees are different, this guide won't tell you how many branches to leave, or buds to cut off. You will decide that yourself, by understanding your tree's needs, and by learning how it will respond to your pruning.

The practice of pruning has a certain mystique, but don't be taken in by this – by observing your own tree(s) and learning a few rules you can become a competent pruner.

This guide is organised into three steps:

Step one – on understanding the features of your tree
Step two – on how a tree responds to various types of pruning
Step three – on deciding what pruning your tree needs and how to do it

Please – resist the temptation to flick through to the most relevant looking diagram. Put down your pruning tools, make a cup of tea and read steps one and two carefully.

Then turn to step three to decide what is best for your tree(s). It is worth learning how an apple tree grows before deciding which bits to cut off.

The principles and techniques described here also apply to pear trees.

Step one: Reading your tree

The first step in understanding your tree is to read its features.

From the tree in winter you can see:

1. the tree's past, including how strongly it grew last year, and the years previous to that
2. its future - whether it will bear many flowers and then fruit this year - or not enough
3. whether it is diseased, or physically injured

Figure 1 shows a branch of apple wood in winter. We can see that it has eight fruit buds, and many smaller, flatter leaf buds. It shows growth rings, which are the scars formed where the top bud was located the previous winter (and also where a leaf bud has grown into a new branch). By looking at the new wood above the highest growth ring we can see how much the branch grew last year. Fruit buds usually develop on wood that is at least a year old, so there are no fruit buds on the part above the last growth ring.

Hopefully, you will be able to identify these features on your apple tree. However, it is likely to look different in other ways, such as the relative amounts of leaf and fruit bud, and the amount of growth in the previous year.

Box 1 Some apple trees are tip bearers, which look a little different, as they have fruit buds on the ends of the twigs. Only a small minority of varieties are tip bearers (though some are partial tip bearers). A tip bearer will show the larger fruit buds at the ends of shoots in winter, and a lack of fruiting side shoots. You can also identify whether yours is one by checking the variety with the nursery, or on the internet.

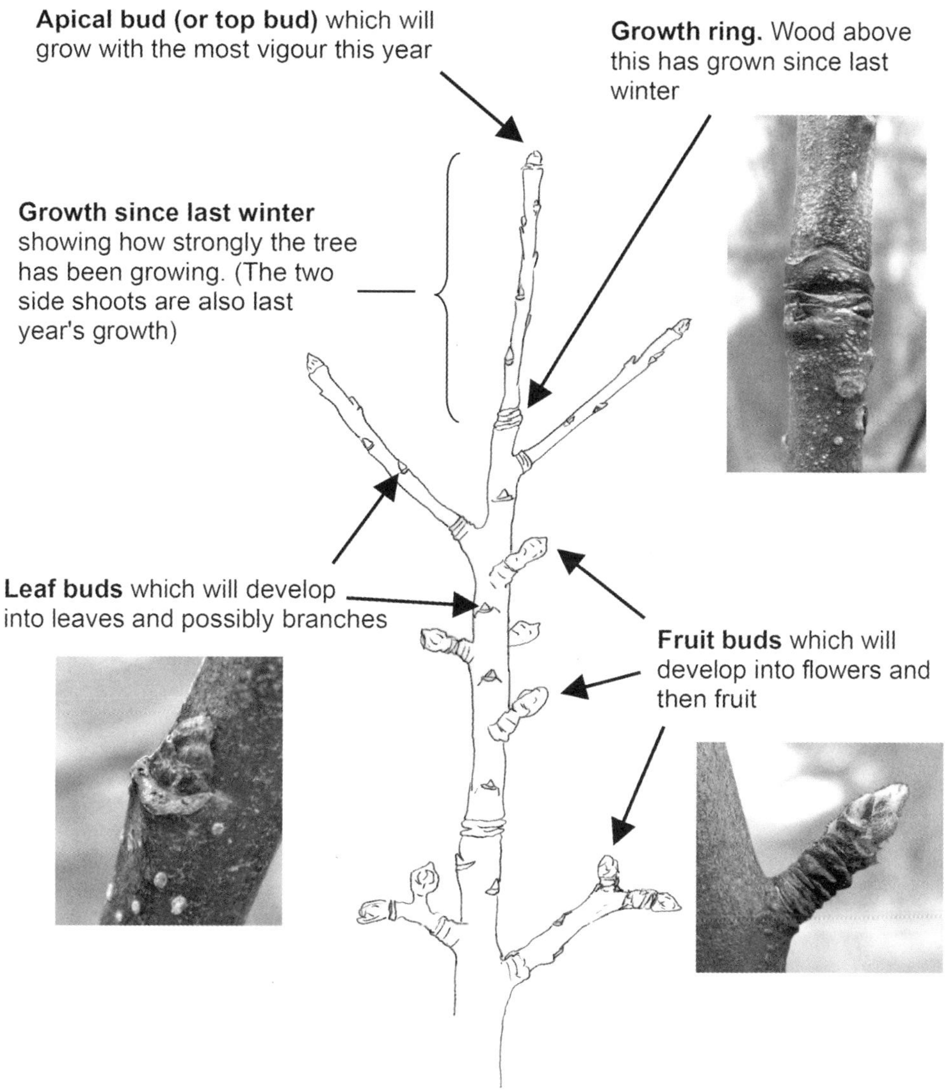

Fig 1 Features of an apple branch in winter

Figure 2 shows a branch that put on very little growth last year. It has had plenty of fruit buds, but the tree is lacking in vigour. The branch shown in figure 3 grew strongly last year, but has no fruit buds. Step two explains how pruning can address these problems.

Fig 2 A weak growing branch. There is little new growth to be seen here. Though there are plenty of fruit buds, they are becoming weak due to the tree's lack of vigour.

Fig 3 A strong branch with no fruit buds. Here we can see plenty of new growth, but no fruit buds.

Box 2 The domesticated apple tree

An apple tree is usually made up of two different individual trees joined together by a 'graft'. The top half of the tree determines the type of fruit produced, as well as other characteristics such as disease resistance. The lower half determines the characteristics of the roots and therefore the vigour of the tree and the size it is likely to grow to.

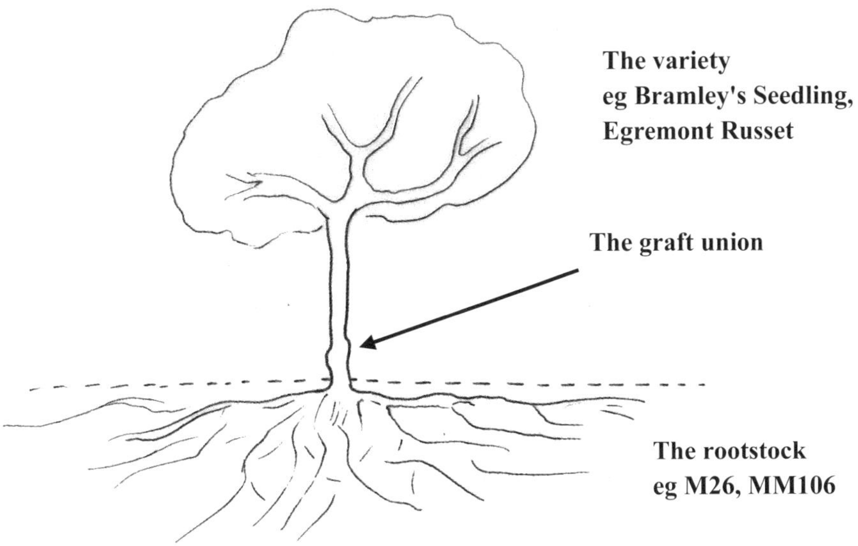

Rootstock	Likely height of tree (metres)
Apple M27	1.5 to 2
Apple M26	2.2 to 3
Apple MM106	3 to 4.5
Apple M111	3.5 to 5
Apple M25	over 4.5
Pear Quince A	2.5 to 3
Pear Quince C	3 to 3.5

Step two: Understanding tree growth

This section explains the principles of tree growth and how a tree responds to different types of pruning cut. We'll then apply this knowledge to pruning our own trees in step three.

Winter pruning

In winter, the tree stores food (made by photosynthesis over the summer) in its roots, ready to be used to make leaves and shoots. In the spring, the sap rises, carrying dissolved food up the tree to the buds. Pruning in winter (when the tree is without leaves) reduces the number of buds, but the tree's food store is retained in the roots. Therefore, if you prune a tree in winter, it will have a surplus of energy to grow more leaves and branches in the spring, and the more you cut off, the more it will grow. Removal of large branches causes the growth of long straight shoots called 'water shoots' from dormant buds, whereas removing the top of a smaller branch or twig causes growth from the remaining highest buds. See figures 4 and 5.

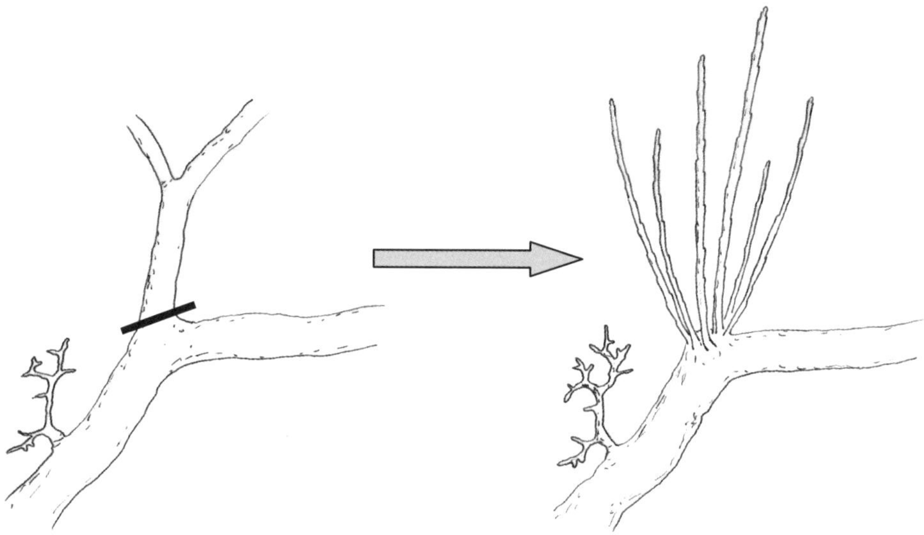

Fig 4 Effect of winter pruning – removal of a whole branch. Removing a branch in winter causes dormant buds to grow, forming new shoots called "water shoots".

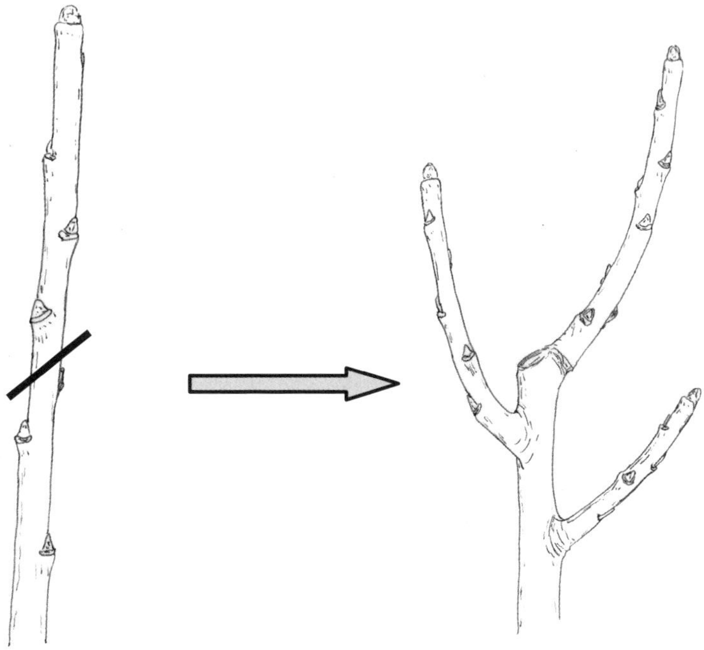

Fig 5 Effect of winter pruning of young wood. Young wood removed in winter causes more growth from the upper-most buds.

Summer pruning

In summer, the tree's energy is mainly in the top half of the tree, in all those lush leaves. Pruning that removes leafy growth will take away sugars, proteins and other substances essential for life. This encourages the tree to go into insurance mode, focusing on the next generation by producing flowers and then apples containing seeds. Therefore, some of the leaf buds will turn into fruit buds. This means that pruning in summer reduces growth, but increases flower and fruit production. The effect of summer pruning can be seen in the winter wood as an increased number of fruit buds – as shown in figure 6.The best time for summer pruning is between late July and September. This is when trained fruit is pruned, keeping the trees in their desired shapes by limiting the branch growth. The later in the season it is done, the less regrowth will occur.

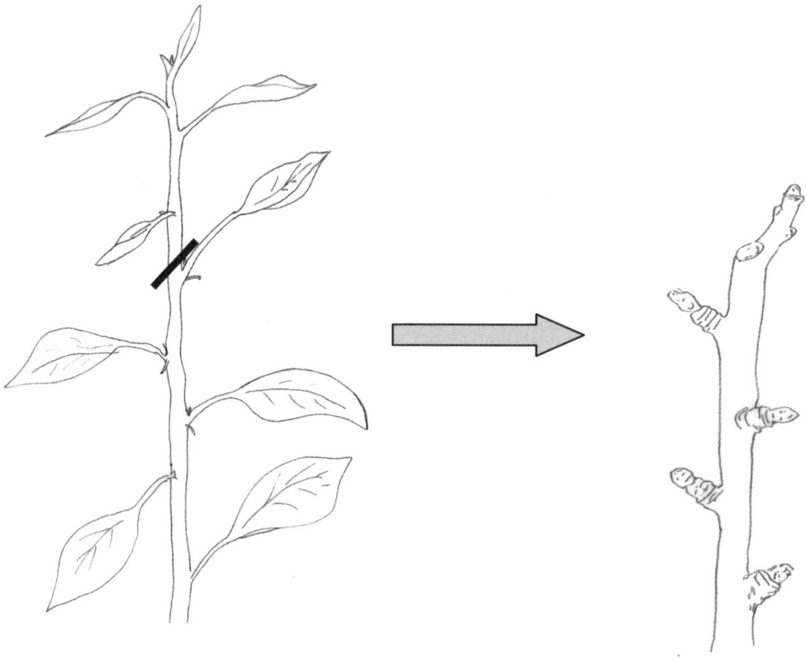

Fig 6 Effect of summer pruning on a young shoot. Removal of leafy growth results in a small amount of re-growth, and the formation of fruit buds.

By appropriate levels of both winter and summer pruning we influence the relative amounts of leaf and fruit buds. Keeping these in balance is important to allow the leaves to produce enough energy by photosynthesis, to support the fruit crop each year.

Bushy and lanky growth

By choosing where and when to make the cuts you can either make your tree bushier or make it more open. Trees have evolved to grow upwards, to out-compete other plants for light. Therefore, the buds higher up the tree send out more growth, and hormones reduce growth from buds further down. If we remove the top bud it disrupts this effect and growth takes place from a number of remaining buds below. Therefore, cutting off the top buds in winter causes branching, as can be seen in the winter pruning shown in figure 5. This effect does not occur so much after summer pruning because the tree does not have surplus energy for formation of new branches, as shown in figure 6. A more open tree can be formed by cutting out whole branches, as explained in step three.

Upright and spreading growth

A tree is more likely to produce fruit buds on growth that is close to the horizontal. Trained fruit takes advantage of this by creating lots of heavy fruiting horizontal or low angled branches.

The direction in which a new shoot grows is determined by the direction that the bud is facing, for example in figure 5, the top shoot grows to the right because the bud is on the right hand side of the twig.

Step three explains how to apply the above principles to pruning your tree.

Box 3

Principles of pruning

- **Pruning in winter promotes leaf and branch growth.**
- **Pruning in summer promotes fruit buds and reduces leaf and branch growth.**
- **Top branches grow more than lower branches, and the top buds of branches grow more than the lower buds.**
- **Removing the top bud causes new branches to grow from lower buds. The new branches will grow in the direction that the buds are facing.**
- **Branches growing more horizontally have less vigour, but more fruit buds.**

Step three: Pruning your tree

For the first few years after planting, an apple tree needs **formative** pruning to create the shape of the tree.

When mature, it will benefit from **maintenance** pruning to give a balance of leaf and fruit production, to remove disease and ensure a healthy spacing of branches.

An old tree can benefit from **restorative** pruning to improve its shape or vigour, or to bring it back into bearing.

In practice, these boundaries are not so clear cut, and your tree is likely to need a combination of the above.

Formative pruning

In tending a young tree, you are the master of its future shape. Most garden apple trees are grown in what is known as a 'bush' shape – the classic picture book apple tree, and this is what is described here (though other tree forms are available). Some trees come ready formed, with their first branches in place, but others, often referred to as 'maidens', are just one long straight branch. Therefore, we need to winter prune to form the first branches. The height of this first pruning cut decides how high the branches will emerge from the trunk, as shown in figure 7.

For a few years after planting, pruning in winter is necessary to ensure a good framework of branches. Cutting the young branches back in winter causes each one to branch out further, forming the tree's future structure. Summer pruning may be useful to remove unwanted branches.

If you planted your tree a few years ago and have not done formative pruning yet, it's not too late. You can still form the tree's shape using a mixture of the techniques shown here, and those explained under 'restorative' pruning.

> **Box 4 It is useful to know what rootstock your tree is on**, because this determines how big it is likely to grow. Rootstocks that form smaller trees, eg M27, need to branch lower down. If growing a large 'standard', eg M25, you may want it to branch very high – up above your head. Trained fruit needs to be on vigorous rootstocks to cope with the energy loss caused by summer pruning. See Box 2, page 9 for info on rootstocks.

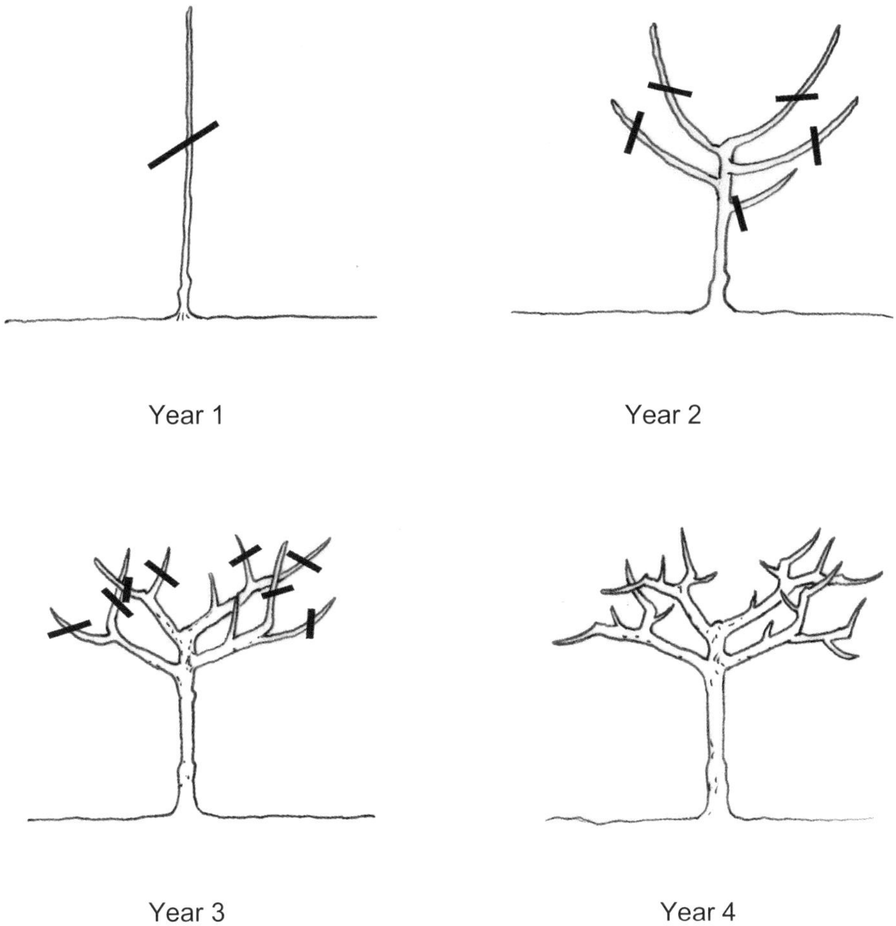

Fig 7 Forming a free-standing tree. The structure of a tree is formed primarily by winter pruning, which causes branching just below the pruning cuts. Summer pruning may be useful to remove or shorten misplaced branches. Here, the two vertical branches in the centre right of the tree have been summer pruned in year 3.

The structure of a trained fruit tree is formed in a similar way, using the effect of winter pruning to cause the growth of new branches, which are then tied into place as needed, as shown in figure 8. Trees can be trained into many different shapes as desired. It is important to form the lower tiers before letting the tree grow branches higher up, due to the tree's tendency to put on most growth on the top branches, leaving little energy for growth lower down.

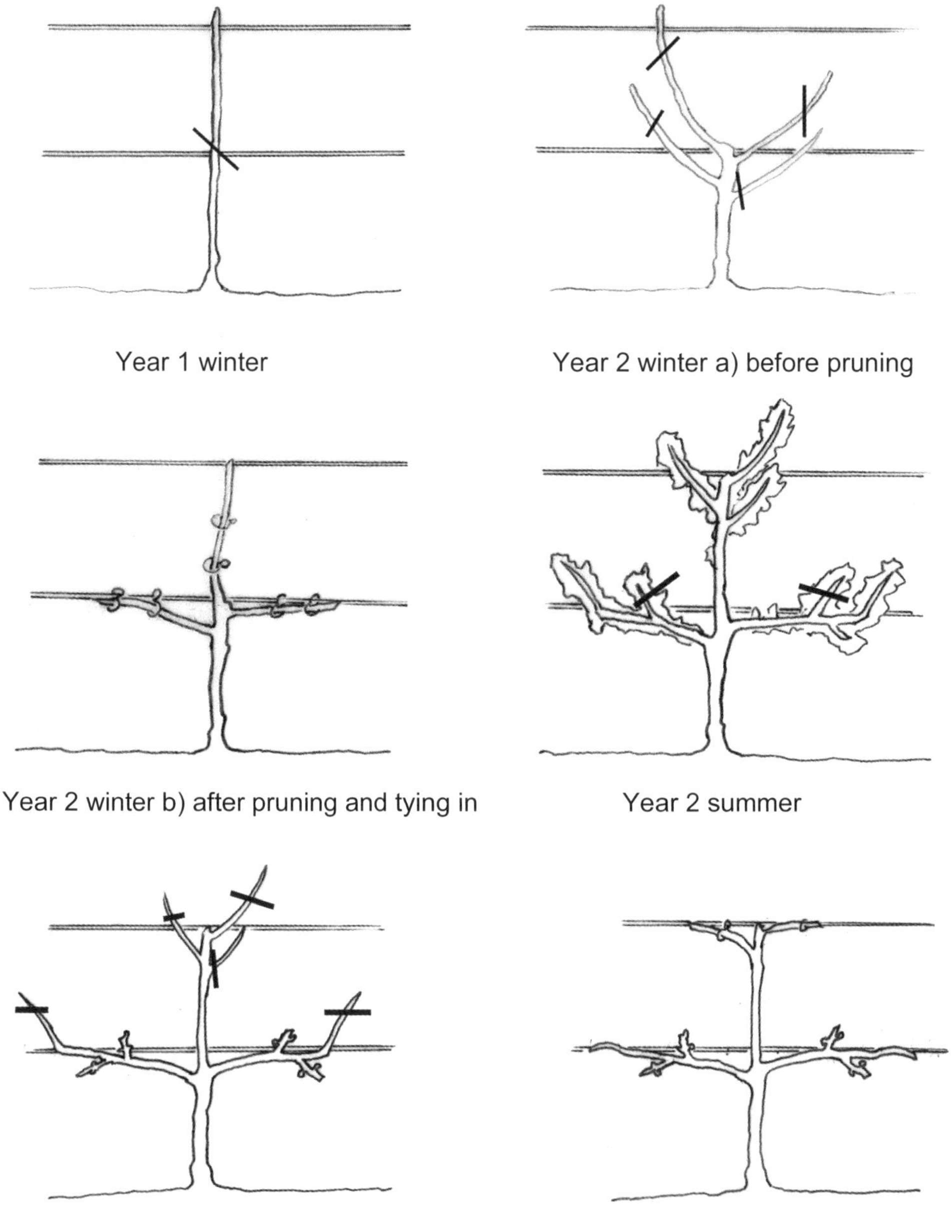

Year 1 winter

Year 2 winter a) before pruning

Year 2 winter b) after pruning and tying in

Year 2 summer

Year 3 winter a) before pruning

Year 3 winter b) after pruning and tying in

Fig 8 Forming a trained tree. Winter pruning is used to form new branches, which are then tied in position. Summer pruning is used to reduce unwanted growth and encourage fruit buds.

Maintenance pruning

When your tree is mature, your pruning will help keep the tree healthy, productive and in good shape.

Look carefully at your tree and decide the following:

1. Does the tree have **canker?**

Fig 9 Canker on apple

Canker is a fungal disease of apple and pear wood (figure 9). If the canker spreads all around the circumference of a branch, it will cause that branch to die off above the wound.

If possible, cut out any canker to well below the diseased part. Some trees, however, are so heavily infected with canker that this is impossible. If this is the case, you'll need to decide whether to let the tree live with the disease as best it can, or remove the tree and start over by planting a more canker-resistant variety. See 'more info', on page 29, for advice on choosing apple varieties. A heavily cankered tree may still live for many years. Many growers recommend disinfecting pruning tools after cutting near canker, with a cloth soaked in alcohol such as surgical spirit, to reduce infection of other trees (or parts of the same tree).

2. Is the growth **crowded**?

They used to say that the branches should be well spaced enough so that you can throw your hat through the tree. Consider whether, when the branches are in full leaf (and hopefully fruit), there will still be space for healthy airflow between them.

The tree may be crowded with long straight '**water shoots**', which are formed after winter pruning as described in step two. Many a tree has endured one or two winter pruning attempts and then been left with no follow up pruning, causing a mass of overgrown long straight branches.

If your tree is too crowded, it is best to cut out whole branches at a joint, as shown in figure 10. Large branches are best removed in winter, as too much summer pruning can weaken the tree. Most of the tree's energy for re-growth will go to the upper parts of the tree, but the cut may cause the formation of some water shoots, which will need be be removed (ideally in summer). Smaller branches can be removed in summer, and this should not result in the formation of water shoots.

Winter pruning to remove branch

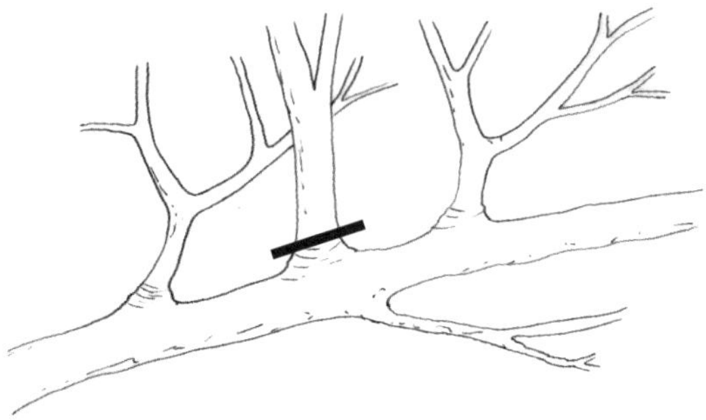

The following winter, showing water shoots

Fig 10 Removal of a branch to make the tree less crowded. This has caused the growth of some water shoots, which need to be removed.

3. Is the growth too **sparse**? Reducing the length of lanky branches in winter will encourage them to bush out as shown in figure 11.

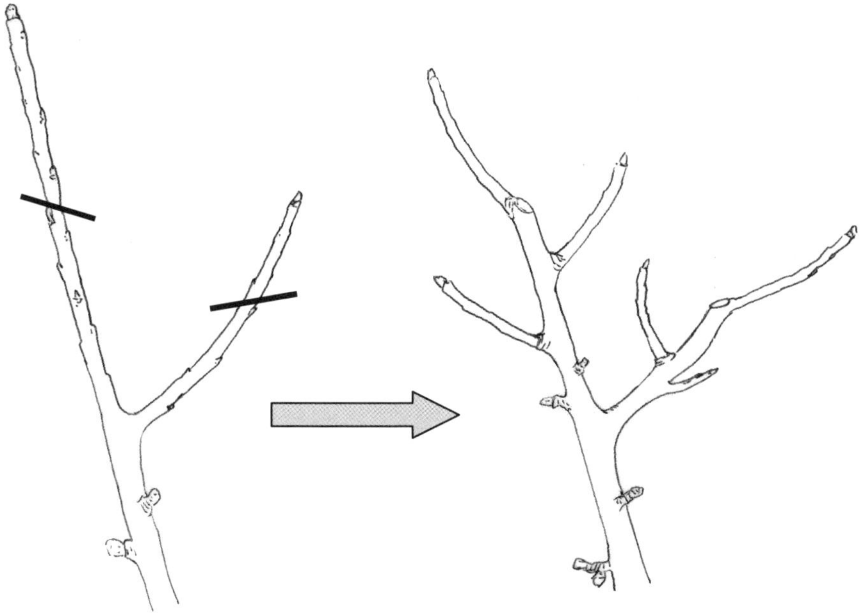

Fig 11 Winter pruning to encourage more bushy growth.

4. Are the branches too **vertical**? If the tree is getting too high and/or not producing enough fruit buds, it will help to create a more spreading shape. Take out the more vertical and central branches, leaving more outward leaning branches, as shown in figure 12. Cutting to an outward facing bud encourages more outward growth. Flexible branches can be tied down to a lower angle as shown in figure 13.

5. Are any branches **crossing** and rubbing against each other? Prune out one of these to prevent physical injury.

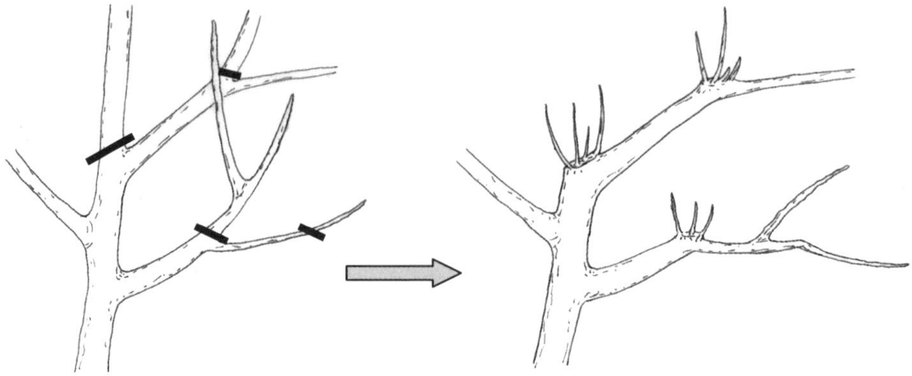

Fig 12 Removal of more upright branches to favour growth at a lower angle. Water shoots will need to be removed (ideally in summer), though some may be retained if suitably placed.

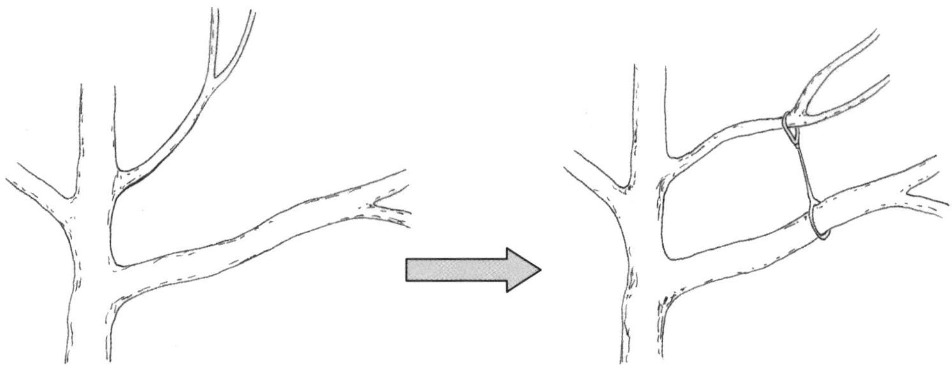

Fig 13 Branches can also be tied down to a lower angle when young and flexible.

6. Has the tree got **many fruit buds and/or too few young strong new shoots?** Thin out some fruiting wood, and cut out some larger branches in winter to encourage new growth. Figure 14 shows an example of this. Regulating the amount of fruit bud can prevent 'biennial bearing' in which trees have a bumper crop one year, but a sparse crop the next. If the tree is growing weakly, check for other causes such as shade, inadequate soil, or a neglected tree tie that may be slowly strangling the trunk.

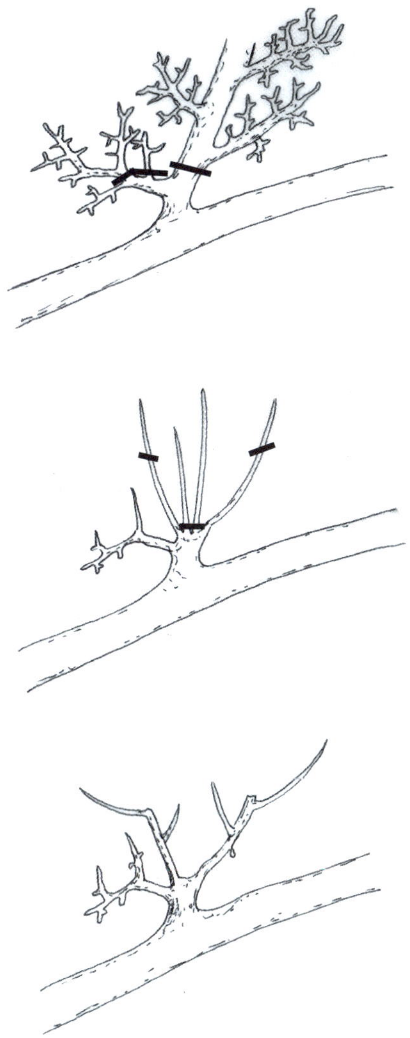

Removal of an old branch with weak, crowded growth.

The following winter, showing water shoots.

The next winter, showing branching to form new, stronger growth.

Fig 14. This branch had become crowded with fruit buds and is lacking in vigour. Taking out crowded growth in winter causes stronger regrowth, which can be used to form a new structure.

7. Does it have **too few fruit buds**? Tie some branches to a lower angle. Form new fruiting wood by cutting back strong shoots in summer as shown in figure 15.

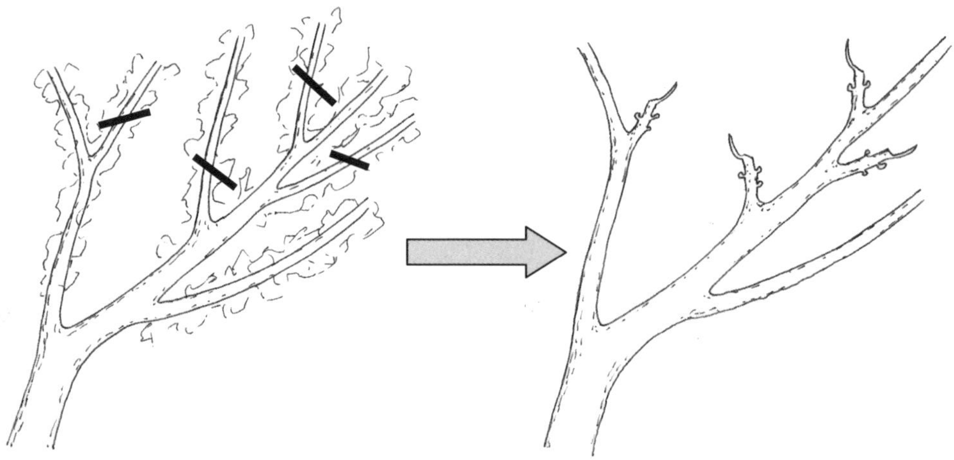

Fig 15 Formation of fruiting wood by summer pruning.

If your tree is a **tip bearer** (see box 1, page 6), which bears fruit on the ends of young shoots, instead of building up fruit buds on side shoots, you need to winter prune so that there are many branch tips. However, be careful not to prune too many branches, or you will remove too many branch tips which carry next year's fruit buds. Partial tip bearers can still be encouraged to fruit on side branches as non tip bearers (or 'spur bearers') do.

8. Is the tree lopsided or leaning? First, check for causes of uneven growth, for example, is the tree too close to a hedge or another tree? If so, you need to decide whether to remove the fruit tree (and re-plant if not too old), or take out or cut back the competitor. Strong winds can also cause leaning and it may be that your tree needs more shelter.

It may be possible to re-stake the tree in a more upright position. Once appropriate action has been taken, growth can be influenced by summer pruning of the vigorous side and winter pruning of the weaker side.

Maintenance pruning of trained fruit

Though most of the checks above are also useful for trained fruit, maintenance pruning mainly consists of summer pruning to remove unwanted leaf and branch growth, as shown in figure 16. Be sure to leave side-shoots long enough for fruit buds to develop on. Occasionally, fruiting wood becomes overgrown, in which case it can be removed in winter and re-formed from the resulting re-growth.

Fig 16. Summer pruning of trained fruit reduces leafy growth and encourages fruit bud formation.

Restorative pruning

Restorative pruning is performed on old trees, that have become out of shape and/or unproductive. It can be a bit of a gamble because not all trees respond well. The drastic pruning required and resulting tender growth can make the tree more prone to disease. Fruit trees do have a life span (which varies according to the rootstock and growing situation) and some trees may just be past it.

There's many an old fruit tree, that is much loved, but not performing well, and it can be hard to decide whether to attempt to restore it. If your tree is an endearing shape and wildlife attractant, then let it be, and be glad when you get fruit. You can put in new trees for fruit production. If you are short of space, consider training the trees so they can fit in smaller spaces.

If you have a very old tree that bears wonderfully tasting fruit of an unknown variety then you could get it identified by sending the fruit to a fruit identification service and then buy and plant a new tree of that variety. Or you can propagate a young tree of the same variety by taking a cutting in winter and getting it grafted by a good plant nursery. See the 'more info' section on page 29 for fruit identification and grafting services.

If your tree is in reasonable health, with good tasting fruit and you are happy to change its shape, then restorative pruning may be the best option.

Restorative pruning usually involves severely cutting back the tree in winter and then re-forming a new framework from the resulting re-growth. It is common for neglected trees to have grown extra branches above the original framework, or new, strongly growing ones from the centre of the tree, as shown in figure 17. These are often too high for easy fruit picking, and can shade out the lower branches. They can be removed in winter so that the original framework remains.

With large trees, the major branch removal is best done over two to three years. If the tree is very out of shape or has no productive wood, it may be necessary to completely form a new framework. In which case, much of the tree is removed and the new framework formed from selecting the best positioned of the resulting water shoots.

Neglected trained fruit often has many large upright branches which have formed where they are not wanted. These can be removed in winter, thus restoring the shape, and new fruiting wood formed from the resulting regrowth.

Before restorative pruning: the tree has large vertical branches shading the lower limbs and fruit is too high for picking.

The following winter: the large, vertical branches have been removed and water shoots have formed.

The next winter: most water shoots have been removed, but some retained and pruned to begin the formation of a new framework.

Fig 17 Restorative pruning showing a tree with extra branches above the original framework, and the process of removal. Branch removal causes growth of water shoots as expected. Though the tree is only shown here in winter, water shoots are best removed in summer, leaving well placed shoots to form the new framework. By reducing the length of these in winter, branching is encouraged and a new structure formed.

Box 5 Cutting techniques

As well as cutting in the right place, it is important to make smooth cuts to prevent moisture collecting, as this can encourage disease.

Damage to the tree is minimised by following these guidelines:

- Always cut just above a bud, as shown in figure 18, or where a branch joins. If you cut mid-way between buds, the part above the bud will die and may attract disease.

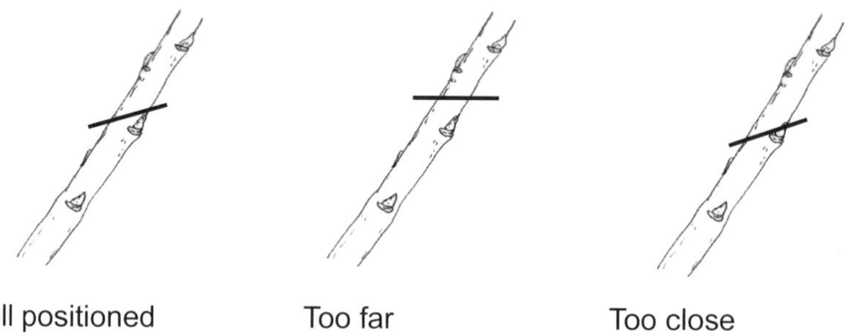

Fig 18 Showing the angle and position of a good pruning cut.

- Use the appropriate size of tool. Forcing a tool can cause the wood to rip.
- When cutting off a large branch, take it off in sections as they are easier to handle and won't cause injury to you or the tree, as shown in figure 19. The final cut should be taken close to the main branch, or trunk, but leaving a slight stump. This enables the wound to heal more easily.

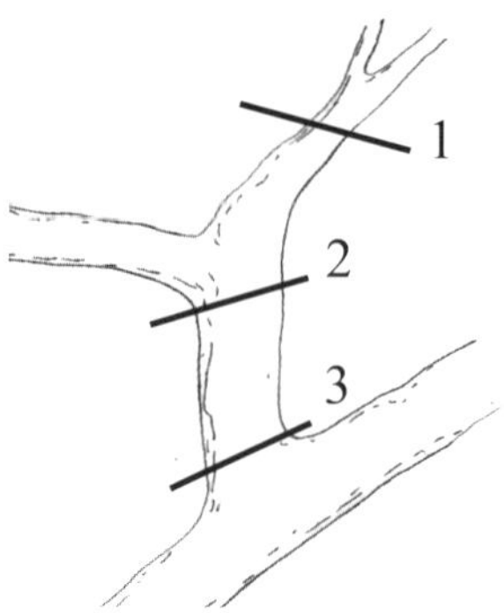

Fig 19
Pruning cuts for removing a large branch.

- For very big trees it may be safer to call in a tree surgeon.

Tools

Your tools don't need to be shiny, but they need to be sharp. Looking after your tools makes pruning more pleasurable, and it is not difficult to do. Figures 20a to 20e show well used, but effective pruning tools. Bow saws and most pruning saws have replaceable blades, so keep a few spares handy and replace when necessary.

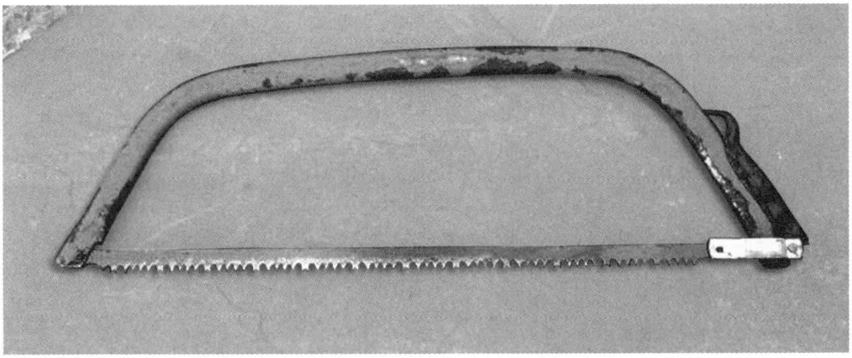

Fig 20a Bow saw – for branches over 3 inches (7cm).

Fig 20b Pruning saw – for branches from ¾ inch (2cm) to 3 inches (7cm).

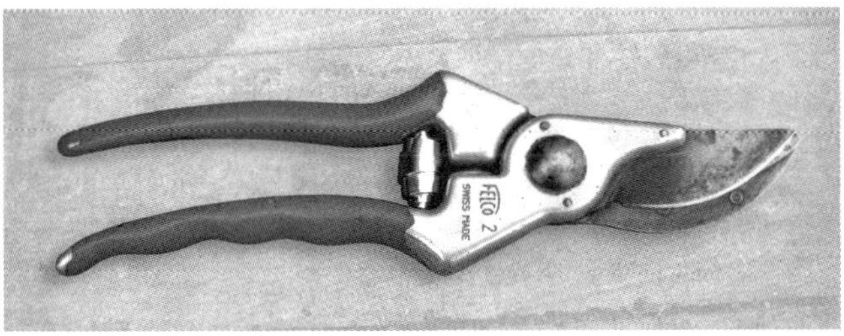

Fig 20c Secateurs – for branches up to ¾ inch (2cm).

'Bypass' secateurs, which have a scissor action, make cleaner cuts than 'anvil' secateurs, which cut against a solid block.

Fig 20d Pruning knife – useful for tidying up messy cuts.

Secateurs and pruning knives can be cleaned with wire wool and sharpened with a small sharpening stone, as shown in figure 20e. Regular oiling of moving parts also keeps them working smoothly.

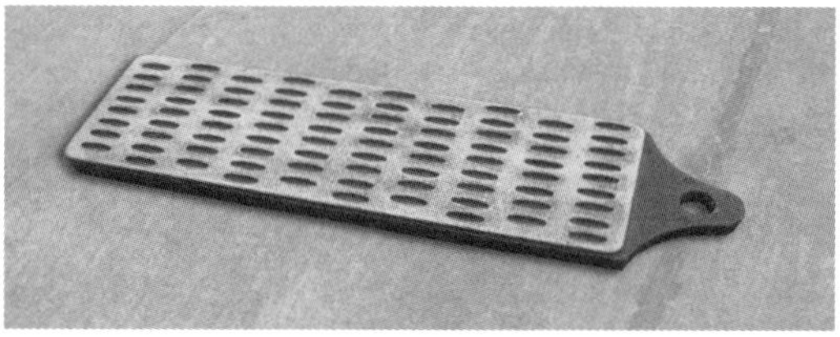

Fig 20e. A 'diamond' sharpening stone (about 8cm by 3cm), which is used for secateur blade and pruning knife sharpening.

Keeping it up

As you become a more skillful pruner, you will find yourself paying more attention to your tree and your pruning will become better judged. Your now well-pruned tree will require less work, as there will be less need for correction of previous mistakes or neglect.

It can, however, be hard at first to get in the habit of observing your tree's growth, especially in summer when there's so much else to do. So, organise a reminder for yourself to have a good look at your trees in July – write it in your diary, or set a mobile phone reminder. Take photos as a record of what you did, and your tree's responses to it.

More information

Here are a few internet resources that may be useful.

Pruning demonstrations

There are many pruning demonstrations on the internet, including those by:

Ian Sturrock and Sons (Welsh fruit tree nursery)
http://www.iansturrockandsons.co.uk/video/pruning.html

Stephen Hayes (Fruitwise Apples)
http://www.youtube.com/watch?v=Q_jqgWXlUHM

Fruit identification

The national apple collection at Brogdale (Kent) will identity an unknown apple variety from a sample of the fruit:
http://www.brogdalecollections.org/fruit-identification/

Grafting services

These nurseries will graft a new tree from a cutting supplied by you:

Orange Pippin Trees
http://www.orangepippintrees.co.uk/articles/fruit-tree-propagation-service

Keepers Nursery
http://www.keepers-nursery.co.uk/bud-grafting-service.htm

Choosing varieties and designing orchards

For information on disease-resistant varieties, and advice on rootstocks, spacing, planting, etc see:

The Royal Horticultural Society
https://www.rhs.org.uk/advice/profile?PID=330

The report 'Growing Fruit in Powys', which can be downloaded from http://www.powysprp.org.uk/uploads/tx_prp/Growing_Fruit_in_Powys_en_Final.pdf or http://www.gerddibroddyfigardens.co.uk/?page_id=332

'Own-root' fruit trees

If you would like to know more about why fruit trees are grafted or how (and why) to grow non-grafted (own-root) fruit trees, see information from:

Orange Pippin Trees
http://www.orangepippintrees.co.uk/articles/own-root-fruit-trees

Cool Temperate Nursery
http://www.cooltemperate.co.uk/own-root-project/